CA Proficiency 1

LAW FOR ACCOUNTANTS (RoI) TOOLKIT

CA Proficiency 1

LAW FOR ACCOUNTANTS (RoI) TOOLKIT

Published by
Chartered Accountants Ireland
Chartered Accountants House
47-49 Pearse Street
Dublin 2
www.charteredaccountants.ie

© Chartered Accountants Ireland 2007, 2009

Copyright of publication rests in entirety with Chartered Accountants Ireland. All rights reserved. No part of this text may be reproduced or transmitted in any form or by any means, including photocopying, Internet or e-mail dissemination, without the written permission of Chartered Accountants Ireland. Such written permission must also be obtained before any part of this document is stored in a retrieval system of any nature.

This publication is designed to provide accurate and authoritative information in regard to the subject matter covered. It is provided on the understanding that Chartered Accountants Ireland is not engaged in rendering professional services. If professional advice or other expert assistance is required, the services of a competent professional should be sought.

ISBN 978-0-903854-86-3

First published 2007
Reprinted with corrections 2009

Typeset by Hurix, India
Printed by ColourBooks, Dublin, Ireland

CONTENTS

Introduction   1

Law   5

Solutions   13

INTRODUCTION

ICAI Examinations – Storylines

Dear Student

As part of the CA Proficiency 1 course you will take on the role of "Chris", a fictitious trainee chartered accountant. Chris's job entails specific responsibilities for three clients, detailed below. As you work through the material in each of the subject-areas, you will be asked to attempt tasks presented to Chris on behalf of each of these clients. These tasks are designed to help you apply the knowledge and skills required for your professional examinations.

You should treat these simulations as though they are real-life tasks. Try to put yourself in Chris's position – consider how you might respond to the client, where you might go to get information and when you might ask for help. While some of the tasks will be completed within the lecture setting, others will be available for you to complete in your own time. Watch out for the signposts on these tasks: often they will refer you to some necessary pre-reading. In addition, the signposts will also note where you can find supplementary questions.

Should you have any suggestions, please let us know. Best of luck with the Toolkit, and with the rest of your studies.

Kind Regards

Joanne Powell
Syllabus Development Manager
joanne.powell@icai.ie

Chris's Background

You are Chris, a trainee accountant with Shield Kenwick, Chartered Accountants & Registered Auditors. Your manager is one of the partners, Mr Ryan. You have just received the following memo from Mr Ryan.

Having agreed to Mr Ryan's suggestions, you return to your desk and continue work.

SHIELD KENWICK
CHARTERED ACCOUNTANTS &
REGISTERED AUDITORS

INTERNAL MEMO

To: Chris
From: Mr Ryan
Date: 12 October 2009
Re: Update following six month review meeting

At your recent review meeting we agreed that you are ready to take on some extra responsibilities and that you should have further direct exposure to clients. I have considered how this might be best achieved, and have decided the following:

Jane Dough – The Dough House

Jane Dough is a new client, starting up a new business. As part of your duties you will be the first point of contact and reference for any queries from Jane. In particular, you will be responsible for the preparation of Jane's books and records, income tax, PAYE and VAT returns. These will be signed off by me in the usual way. I have included background notes on Jane in Appendix 1. Jane also mentioned that she is interested in the activities of a local producers group, called Poulenc Partnership. I have included their details in Appendix 2, in case you require them at a later point.

MCL Limited

As part of your duties, you have been seconded one day per week as assistant management accountant to a busy manufacturing company that is a client of the firm. Shield Kenwick provides general support and advice, along with accounting and taxation services, to this client. We do not carry out the statutory audit. The company, MCL Limited, is family owned and you will report directly to the Finance Director, Mike Smithers, while at the office. Additionally, I would hope that you will come directly to me with specific queries which you would like to discuss. I have included some basic background information on MCL in Appendix 3.

I anticipate that these responsibilities should help to address some of the areas of concern we had in relation to the competencies identified in the Online CA Diary. I suggest we keep the process under review over the next six to 12 months.

Appendix 1: Jane Dough – The Dough House

On 1 January 2009, Jane Dough established a new business, a coffee and pastry shop, known as "The Dough House". In the future, Jane hopes to also sell local pottery and produce on a small scale. Jane has identified suitable premises in a busy part of town which do not appear to be particularly well serviced by coffee and pastry shops. While Jane has extensive experience working in a coffee shop environment, having been assistant manager in a similar shop for several years, she has never owned or run her own business before.

On 1 January 2009, Jane withdrew €/£5,000 from her own savings and her husband John's great-aunt gave her €/£10,000 as a gift to put towards opening The Dough House. Jane opened a separate bank account for The Dough House, lodging €/£14,500 to the account and retaining €/£500 as petty cash. Jane then signed the deeds on The Dough House's new premises, which were for sale at €/£50,000, drew down a mortgage with a local building society for €/£45,000 and paid the balance due for the premises from the business's new bank account. The mortgage is repayable over 20 years and the repayments, which are due at the end of each month, are fixed at €/£250 per month.

While Jane had taken redundancy from her previous employer, the redundancy payment is not expected for some months due to circumstances outside her control.

Jane will need help at lunchtimes and weekends in The Dough House, and her nephew and niece have agreed to help, so long as they are paid in cash. They are 14 and 17 respectively. Additionally, Jane's husband John has agreed to help whenever possible. Jane is uncertain whether or not she needs to register as an employer.

Jane and John have two young children, and her husband's incapacitated great-aunt lives with them. John is not employed as he cares for their two children on a full-time basis at home. However, he does have an interest in some rental properties and a small share portfolio. Jane and John have always tried to save a percentage of their income and these savings are kept in a variety of accounts: Credit Union account, deposit account and SSIA (now matured). In addition, Jane and John each have a personal pension, life assurance (with critical illness), permanent health insurance (PHI) and are members of VHI.

Appendix 2: The Poulenc Partnership

The Poulenc Partnership is a group of artisans who make and sell local produce and crafts through farmers' markets, seasonal fairs and independent coffee shops. The partnership has been in existence for approximately eight years and there are currently five partners. The partners share all income and costs, with individual products being sold into the partnership at an agreed price and then sold on to third parties. The current partnership structure is as follows:

- Maire Louise Phillips (25%) – potter and clay-worker;
- Joseph Phillips (father of Maire Louise) (15%) – basket weaver;
- Christopher Pringle (20%) – food producer (preserves, cakes, biscuits etc) using local ingredients;
- Caiti Pollen (25%) – craft worker (jewellery from local materials and wrought iron items (candlesticks, tables, fire irons etc); and
- Ellen Peterson (15%) – public relations and marketing professional, and the only partner who draws a salary.

While Joseph Phillips hopes to retire during 2010, he may continue to sell some of his baskets to the partnership.

Jane has been invited to join The Poulenc Partnership, with effect from 1 July 2008, purchasing Joseph Phillips' 15% interest in return for an investment of €/£50,000.

As The Poulenc Partnership is now a client of the firm, Jane has deferred making a decision about joining the partnership until its accounts for the year ended 31 December 2007 have been finalised.

The existing partners have indicated that there are plans to review the partnership structure at the end of 2010.

Appendix 3: MCL Limited

MCL Limited is a large, privately-owned company. It was founded in the 1970s by Matthew Smithers and is still owned by the Smithers family. There has been no change in the ordinary share capital of the company for a number of years and the shareholdings are as follows:

Current Member	Role	Shareholding
Matthew and Maureen Smithers	Founders	8%
Matthew jnr	CEO	22%
Michael	Finance Director	22%
Martina	Production Director	22%
Millie	Sales and Marketing Director	22%
Mervin (based in New York)	not involved in the company	4%

Matthew jnr, Michael, Martina and Millie are the only children of Matthew and Maureen. There are no other directors.

MCL is a textiles company that is involved in producing standard fabric dyes and weaving natural fibre fabrics for use in a variety of home furnishings. The dyes produced are used to dye yarns in-house (but could also be sold directly to third parties). The majority of the woven fabrics are exported to the UK and mainland Europe. However, there is also a core Irish market.

MCL has a large work force which includes: general operatives; weavers (general and skilled); stores team; administration team; and sales and distribution team. Although the company has performed well in the past, it has come under increasing pressure in the last two years.

LAW

The student should be aware of the three major sources of Irish law. Ireland has a common law system, i.e. it is largely based on decisions made by the courts. This is also known as case law or precedent. The second major source of Irish law is legislation, i.e. written laws passed by the Oireachteas. Legislation is also known as statute law or "Acts". The Constitution of 1937 is also a source of law, but with little direct impact on business law.

The Irish Courts System is divided into two distinct spheres – civil and criminal. In the civil courts, the remedies usually available to a wronged individual are damages (in the form of monetary compensation) or injunctions (i.e. orders compelling or forbidding certain activities). The remedies available in the criminal courts range from fines to imprisonment with a series of other remedies such as probation orders, compensation orders etc.

Each court has its own jurisdiction, i.e. it can deal with certain types of cases, based on monetary limits and the geographical area of the court. Minor cases involving lesser monetary claims or summary crimes are dealt with in the District Court. More serious cases are dealt with in the Circuit Court, and the High Court deals with cases involving civil claims exceeding circa €38,000 or in the criminal sphere, serious crimes such as rape, murder or treason. All courts may interpret legislation, but the High Court can declare an act to be unconstitutional i.e. null and void.

The Supreme Court is an appellate court that hears appeals on points of law (i.e. the cases are not reheard by the court, rather, a technical point is being argued). Also, the student should also be aware of the existence of the Special Criminal Court – this court operates without a jury and deals with subversive crimes, for example serious drug trafficking and terrorist related offences.

Broadly speaking, you should be aware of the many issues that arise in the set of circumstances as outlined above. You should understand and recognise legal/ethical issues as such. You should understand, in general terms, the following:

- Ethical issues surrounding the student's ability to advise the client in conjunction with the responsible partner in the firm.
- Company/Commercial Law: that is the various types of business vehicles open to the client to use in furtherance of the business venture, namely, sole tradership, partnership

or limited liability company and the legal ramifications of each, share and loan capital, company administration and directors' responsibilities.
- Contract law, essential elements of contracts, postal rule, key elements of contract for sale, termination of contracts.
- Landlord and Tenant law, short-term leases/long-term leases and the ramifications of each of these types of leases, terms and conditions contained in leases, full repair and insuring leases, landlord's responsibilities and tenant's responsibilities. Planning law and its ramifications.
- Employment law, employer's obligations towards employees, employment contracts (difference between contracts of service versus contracts for services), the effect of employment legislation as far as employee's rights are concerned, ages at which employees are entitled to commence work and whether there are exceptions in relation to family members.
- Data Protection legislation: main provisions of the Data Protection Act 1988 to 2003 (DPA 1988-2003).
- Health and Safety law and the obligation of employers to ensure that they provide a safe place to work and safe systems of work.
- Tax law and the ramifications of setting up a business and the requirement to register for VAT, PAYE, PRSI, etc. (The detail of these registrations will be assessed under the Taxation course.)

NB
P = Plaintiff
D = Defendant
CA = Companies Act

Meeting 1 – 1 January 2009

Mr Ryan has just called you into the office. Jane Dough has left a message stating that she is going to call in this afternoon to pick up the forms she needs to register her "company". Mr Ryan has a prior commitment and cannot reach Jane on the phone. He is concerned that she is making the wrong decision, but knows from experience that Jane can be quite strong-willed. He plans to *fully* brief her on the issues involved in registering a company (without giving her the forms); and to flag that there are other options available and that these should be considered. In prepare for this, he has asked you to write a very detailed briefing note for Jane which covers the following in relation to limited companies:

- Registration procedure – Memorandum and Articles of Association and Form A1, promoters, object clauses, the *Ultra Vires* doctrine, types of companies, characteristics of a registered company.

He wants to make sure Jane understands the full implications of registering a company, plans to add the following cover letter anything his concerns to the briefing note and suggests that Jane makes an appointment to talk to him.

> **SHIELD KENWICK**
> **CHARTERED ACCOUNTANTS & REGISTERED AUDITORS**
>
> Ms Jane Dough
> 11 Harbourville Road
> Ballymack
>
> Dear Ms Dough
>
> Further to your call this morning I attach a detailed briefing note that outlines the various issues to be considered when registering a limited company.
>
> It should also be noted that there are other possibilities open to you, which may be more suitable to your circumstances than registering as a limited company. You may have already discussed these with your legal advisors, but if not I would be very happy to meet with you early next week and review the possibilities. My secretary will be happy to make an appointment which is convenient for you.
>
> In the meantime, should you have any queries, please do not hesitate to contact me.
>
> Yours sincerely
> Mr Ryan

Task 1

Prepare the briefing note required by Mr Ryan. He will review the note before you leave it out for Jane to collect.

Phonecall – early January 2009

Jane has phoned you and asked if you would have time to prepare a note for her. Following her study of the briefing paper you prepared for her, she is now unsure whether she should be setting up as a limited company. She is very much aware of her lack of specific business skills or expertise, and has noted that whilst she has been an assistant manager in a business in a related area, this is entirely different to running the business herself. She asks you to explain what the term "sole trader" means, and whether there are any advantages to operating in this way.

Task 2

Draft a memo to Jane that answers her questions and suggests where she might access further information if required.

Meeting 2 – January 2009

Jane has met with Mr Ryan, and has decided to set up as a sole trader. She has filled in the requisite forms and has commenced trading. She mentions that she has been speaking with some members of a local craft partnership and is interested in the possibility of joining with them at a later date (perhaps during 2010). Jane has learned that it is better to be advised "up front", before any key decisions are taken, and would like you to advise generally in relation to partnerships and how they are formed. In particular, she would like you to explain the following:

- Definition of "Partnership" with regard to the relevant legislation
- Partnership Agreement or "Deed of Partnership" and its contents
- Liability of Partners
- Dissolution of Partnerships
- Types of partners

Task 3

Write a briefing note for Jane which deals with her queries on partnerships.

Meeting 3 – January 2009

Jane has been thinking about her position in relation to her family and their employment by the business, and is anxious to be compliant with the law in relation to (employment) contracts and Health and Safety. She has asked you to advise on contracts she might arrange for her employees to sign in order for her to be compliant with Irish employment law. Also, she is keen to be made aware of any particular provisions of Irish employment law by which she must abide to be compliant in relation to the proposed employment of her nephew (aged 14) and niece (aged 17).

Task 4

Prepare a memo for Jane giving an overview of employment contracts and details of the minimum contents required therein. Include a reference to Health and Safety requirements also.

Task 5

Draft a letter to Jane outlining the specific matters to be considered when employing "young persons" for Mr Ryan to review and sign.

Phone call Mike Smithers – January 2009

Mike Smithers has just been on the phone. MCL's office cleaner is employed on a temporary contract, and this is due to expire next month. The cleaner comes to the office for three hours every Tuesday and Friday evening. MCL purchases its own cleaning supplies and has its own cleaning equipment (vacuum cleaner, floor polisher etc). The cleaner wants to be paid "cash" and Mike reckons that if he terminates the cleaner's employment and then gets them to sign an invoice every week, that he can treat them as "self-employed". Mike believes that this is a win/win situation, as he also avoids employers' PRSI (legitimately, he believes). He has asked you to check it out.

Task 6

Draft a memo to Mike outlining the difference between contracts for services vs contracts of services. Include a mention of permanent and temporary employment contracts, and the provisions of the Unfair Dismissals Acts when it comes to terminating and rehiring staff within a short space of time.

Meeting 4 – Early February 2009

Jane has asked you generally about Landlord and Tenant law and the position in relation to her lease. She has asked you about the impact of signing a lease and whether there are planning considerations to her using the premises as a coffee shop. She is aware that specific legal advice needs to be sought from her solicitor, but is hoping you can give her a "heads up" in anticipation of this.

Task 7

Draft a memo to Jane that notes the following:

- Brief explanation of a lease
- Overview of the implications of a lease that lasts longer than five years
- Overview of Stamp Duty requirements (in general)
- Potential planning requirements

Meeting 5 – February 2009

Mr Ryan has called you aside. He mentions that Mike Smithers from MCL is concerned about data protection, particularly in relation to the personal data they hold about employees. Mr Ryan plans to meet Mike to discuss the broad issues, and would like you to prepare a file note that could serve as the basis for discussion at this meeting.

Task 8

Draft a file note for Mr Ryan that he can use as the basis for discussion with Mike, which lists (in broad terms) the guidelines MCL should adhere to in relation to employee data.

Meeting 6 – 18 February 2009

Jane calls to your office and proposes that her business will become involved in entering into contracts with suppliers for equipment. She has asked you to describe the main elements of a contract for her, as it is an area with which she is not familiar. Her focus is on needing to know when a contract becomes "binding".

Task 9

Draft a briefing note for Jane that lists and describes the main elements of a contract and focuses on when a contract becomes enforceable.

Internal Meeting – February 2009

Mr Ryan, approaches you with a query pertaining to the Chartered Accountants Regulatory Board's (CARB) complaints process. He has learned from a colleague that Jane Dough has had several chartered accountants firms advising her over the past two years and has fallen out with each of them, leading to complaints being lodged with CARB, the operationally independent body established to oversee the regulation and discipline of ICAI members. He is nervous that Jane Dough may lodge a complaint on the basis of her previous history. He plans to ask the legal department to review the issues, and asks you to draft a memo on his behalf, noting the areas for the legal department to focus on.

Task 10

Draft an internal memo to the legal department, stating the issues you believe they should cover before briefing Mr Ryan on the operation of CARB.

Meeting Friday, week 2 – February

Chris has been asked by Mr Smithers, the director to whom he reports in MCL Limited, to prepare a brief for the other directors in MCL Limited pertaining to how the company Limited can raise funds, and furnishes Chris a written note in this regard. The Mr Smithers director further wishes to know how to properly go about appointing new directors (and removing old directors, if necessary!) together with other miscellaneous queries. The memo is set out as follows:

MEMO

Chris

MCL wishes to raise funds to capitalise its business and I require to be brought up to speed in this regard and require to know how to raise more capital for MCL Limited.

As you know, we have recently appointed new directors to the board and are in the process of inviting more new directors to join the board. This may necessitate the removal/retirement of existing directors. I am also looking into appointing a new Company Secretary.

The auditors are causing me some concern, and I require to be updated in relation to the Office of Auditor as we may have to replace them.

Specifically, please prepare briefs for presentation to the board covering the following points:

- Company Capital: Share Capital v Loan Capital
- The various types of share capital
- The various types of shares that can be issued and the characteristics attaching to each share
- Types of directors
- Appointment and removal of directors
- Company Secretary and his/her responsibilities
- The Office of Auditor, his/her responsibilities, powers and duties and procedure for removal and appointment

Kind regards

Mike Smithers
Finance Director MCL Limited

Task 11

Prepare the brief on company capital and include a note on the types/ characteristics of the shares that can be issued.

Task 12

Prepare a brief on directors, to cover types of directors and the appointment and removal of directors.

Task 13

Prepare the brief required on company secretaries.

Task 14

Prepare the brief required on the Office of Auditor.

SOLUTIONS

Task 1: Response

Briefing Note

To: Jane Dough
From: Shield Kenwick
Re: Issues arising in Company Formation

Company Formation

A registered company is formed by the registration of certain documents with the Companies Registration Office, as required by the CA 1963-2009. The typical Irish company is a small family business with shareholders/directors formed to take advantage of limited liability, and trade as a private company. To incorporate such a company, documents must be prepared and lodged with the Companies Registration Office (CRO), located in Parnell Square and presided over by the Registrar of Companies together with the appropriate fee. Anyone who wishes to register a company is advised to engage the services of a solicitor/chartered accountant in this regard. Under no circumstances should they attempt to set up a company without such professional advice.

Promoters

The person who forms the company is known as the promoter – in these circumstances, it would be you. A promoter is defined by case law in ***Twycross v. Grant* (1877)** as "... one who undertakes to form a company with reference to a given project and to set it going, and who takes the necessary steps to accomplish that purpose". Essentially, promoters are the people who associate together to bring about the formation of a company.

The promoters are agents of the company and owe a fiduciary duty to the company – this duty requires them to act in good faith and in the best interest of the company being formed.

The Registration Procedure

You, as promoter, will need to assist your professional advisors to prepare the documentation necessary for incorporation and present these documents to the Registrar of Companies, together with the appropriate fee. If everything is in order then the Registrar issues a Certificate of Incorporation. The incorporation is advertised in *Iris Oifigiuil* (an official government publication used for making information public) within a period of six weeks. The documents that require registration are:

(a) The Memorandum of Association,
(b) The Articles of Association, plus
(c) Form A1.

Memorandum of Association

A Memorandum of Association must be delivered to the Registrar of Companies before incorporation can take place. This document is equivalent to the company's charter/constitution and seeks to regulate the affairs of the company vis-á-vis the public. A company's memorandum is said to be for external use, i.e of interest to people outside the company. Essentially, it enables a person who invests in the company, or creditors dealing with the company, to ascertain certain basic information concerning the business enterprise.

According to section 6, CA 1963 there are five obligatory clauses that must be contained in the Memorandum of Association. These are:

(a) Name Clause This clause states the name of the company. A name may be refused registration if it is considered undesirable by the Minister for Enterprise, Trade and Employment (section 21 CA 1963). A name will be considered undesirable if:
 (i) It is an offensive or blasphemous name,
 (ii) It suggests or implies a connection with any Government department, local authority or State agency,
 (iii) It uses "bank, society, co-operative or insurance" in its name, unless it has obtained the appropriate permission from the Minister,
 (iv) It includes a registered trademark, without production of the consent of its owner,
 (v) It is regarded as being misleading, or
 (vi) It is the same or very similar as the name of an existing company.

An appeal to a refusal to register a particular name can be made to the High Court.

To ensure that persons dealing with a company know of its nature, section 6 CA 1963 states that if the company is a Public Limited Company then the company name must end with the words Public Limited Company, plc or the Irish equivalent. The relevant Minister is empowered to dispense with this requirement if the company is incorporated for the promotion of commerce, art, science, religion, charity or other useful purpose, and where the company's profits will be used for the promotion of its objectives. Examples include the Irish Cancer Society and the Zoological Gardens of Ireland.

Section 114 CA 1963 requires that the company's name must be displayed at its office or affixed to the outside of their place of business, engraved on the company seal and mentioned in all of the company's business documents (letters, notices, cheques, invoices and receipts). The use of a company's name in an incorrect form may render the directors personally liable for the debts of the company.

Where a company, through inadvertence or otherwise, registers a name that is similar to a company already in existence, the Minister can compel that company to change its name (section 23 CA 1963) within six months of registration. If a company registers a name that is likely to cause confusion with a pre-existing company or trademark, the company may commit the tort (civil wrong) of passing off. An action for passing off may result in an order to change the offending company name, and an award of damages. The statute of limitation for passing off action is six years.

In *Ewing v. Buttercup Margarine Company Limited* [1917] the plaintiff trading as Buttercup Dairy Company obtained an injunction to restrain the defendant from using a similar name, as this could lead to confusion between the two businesses.

At any time in its business life, a company may change its name by a special resolution (75%) of the shareholders, together with the consent of the Minister.

When advising a client on a choice of company name, the availability of the relevant domain name should be considered before the company name is finalised.

(b) Objects Clause The objects of a company are the company's aims – what the company was set up to do. A company may have any legal activity as its objects. A company is not permitted to enter into any transactions that go beyond its objects – this is known as the doctrine of *ultra vires*. All such transactions are null and void. If, for example, a company that has as its main object clothes manufacturing enters into the business of house building and the object of house building, is not provided for in the objects clause as one of the company's objects, then under the traditional doctrine of *ultra vires*, any house building contracts entered into by the company may be deemed *ultra vires*.

In addition to objects a company will also have powers. Powers are ways of achieving the objects. A company's powers may be expressed in the objects clause, but they may also be implied. Objects are specific to a company, but powers are common to all companies, e.g. the power to borrow, to buy and sell etc.

The Companies Consolidation and Reform Bill 2007(CC RB 2007) will make major changes to Irish company law, when it is enacted. A private limited company will be granted the same legal capacity as natural persons, thus objects clauses will not be needed and the *ultra vires* rule will not longer be relevant. (PLCs and companies limited by guarantee will be required to retain objects clauses and will still be subject to the *ultra vires* rule.)

(c) Liability Clause The Liability Clause is simply a declaration stating that the liability of the members (shareholders) is limited. This means that shareholders' liability to pay the debts of the company is limited to any unpaid amounts on their shares. Once shares are paid for in full, shareholders have no further liability for company debts, due to the separate legal personality of the company (see later). Limited liability is the great advantage to forming a limited company.

This privilege may be lost if members of a public company fall below seven and the remaining members continue to carry on business for a period of six months after that event, then every member who knows that the company is operating at the reduced membership becomes liable for all the debts incurred at that time. Limited liability may also be lost where it is proved that members, and others, knowingly carried on the business with an intent to defraud the company's creditors, or for any other fraudulent purpose.

(d) Capital Clause This clause states the amount of the share capital (authorised and issued) with which the company is registered and its division into shares of fixed amounts. If the company is a public limited company the minimum authorised share capital must be at least €38,012.00, of which a quarter must be paid up.

If the company is an unlimited company then the memorandum may omit the capital and limitation of liability clause.

(e) Association/Subscription Clause The subscribers to the company are the first shareholders. Subscribers must state that they desire to form a company and that they agree to take the number of shares set opposite their names. No subscriber to the memorandum may take less than one share. The memorandum must also be signed by all the subscribers, and must contain the subscriber's name, address and the number of shares they are taking in the company. The names of the company's first directors and secretary are also contained in this clause. All subscription signatures must be witnessed.

The Memorandum may be altered to take account of changes in the company. Both the name and the objects clause may be altered by a special resolution (75%) of company members and with the consent of the Minister. If more than 15% of company shareholders or debenture holders object to an alteration they can make an application to the High Court within 21 days of the vote to cancel the alteration. The capital clause may only be altered in accordance with the Articles of Associations and rules set down by the Companies Acts 1963-2009(CA 1963-2009). The limited liability clause may be altered to change the company from limited status to unlimited status, by obtaining the written consent of all the members of the company. All changes to the Memorandum must be notified to the Registrar of Companies within a designated time period.

Articles of Association

This document regulates the internal arrangements and management of the company and is often referred to as the company's rule book. They are referred to as being for internal use, i.e. really only of interest to the members of the company. The articles are inferior to the memorandum and cannot include any provisions that contravene any principal of law or provision in the memorandum. The rules and regulations of the articles deal with such things as:

(a) Shares The issue and transfer of shares, the payment of shares and whether they are partly or wholly paid, whether shares have been or can be issued at a discount, whether shares have been or can be issued at a premium, provisions regulating the share premium account/bonus issues/preliminary expenses/redemption premiums, details of the types of shares issued i.e. ordinary or preference, cumulative or non-cumulative, redeemable or non-redeemable.

(b) Share Capital procedure for altering the share capital as follows:
  (i) by issuing new shares,
  (ii) by converting paid-up stock into shares,
  (iii) by re-converting stock into shares,
  (iv) by consolidating shares,
  (v) by cancelling some of the authorised but not issued share capital.

Note: any alteration of the share capital requires a prior application to the High Court for approval. This alteration will be accepted or rejected by taking into consideration the company's creditors, shareholders and debenture holders.

It may also include details of the amount of authorised and issued share capital, whether it is wholly paid-up, provisions for calling up uncalled share capital, and provisions relating to reserved share capital.

(c) Meetings The procedure to be adopted in relation to the calling of general meetings, the purpose of company meetings and how these meetings should be properly conducted, provisions relating to the frequency of these meetings, arrangements re AGMs, and the procedure to be followed to call an extraordinary GM.

(d) Voting Rights attached to the various classes of company shares.

(e) Directors Provisions relating to the appointment and removal of directors, their powers and duties, home things act as paid servants/agents of the company, as follows:
  (i) nature of their duty is intermittent i.e. they do not have to attend all meetings, but must attend as regularly as is reasonably possible,
  (ii) fiduciary duties to company i.e. to act *bona fide* in the best interests of the company, to avoid conflict of interest situations, accountable for breach of trust, and
  (iii) not bound to give continuous attention to affairs of the company.

(f) Secretary appointments, removal, powers and duties. Company law provides for the appointment of a Company Secretary who has certain obligations under the law. The Articles of Association will usually provide for the procedure for the appointment of the secretary, Form A1 being the document which will appoint the First Secretary.

The secretary has certain responsibilities, that, depending on the terms of the Articles of Association, will include the maintenance of various company registers. All correspondence to a company may be addressed to the Company Secretary.

(g) Payment of dividends Dividends are monetary entitlements that attach to shares and entitle the owner of a share to a certain proportion of the profits of the company. How much dividend a shareholder will receive will depend on the number of shares held and the particular rights attaching to those shares. It will be up to the Board of Directors to declare dividends which will then be divided amongst the various shareholders according to the rights attaching to each particular share. It is not unusual for a Board not to declare a dividend and decide to plough the profits back into the company.

(h) Accounts and Audits Procedures to be adopted in relation to all monies expended/received, purchases and sales, assets and liabilities, the right of directors to inspect the books of accounts, the requirement that they must be lodged with the Companies Registrar within 18 months of incorporation or within one calendar year, and ancillary filing requirements of the Companies Registration Office. As regards auditors, provisions regarding their appointment and duties, reporting to members at the AGM, the procedures to be adopted in relation to preparing reports, sending them to the company secretary, reading them at the AGM, the fact that the report must contain a statement that the company's accounts represent a "true and fair" view of financial affairs of the company, auditors' rights of access to company accounts, and their liability for fraudulent/negligent performance of their duties.

(i) The procedure to be followed in the event of **company liquidation** (both voluntary and involuntary).

(j) Company Borrowing This must be expressly or implicitly permitted by the Memorandum of Association, provisions relating to the granting of fixed charges on the company's assets (a mortgage on a particular piece of property that then may not be sold without the prior consent of the chargeholder) and floating charges (a mortgage on circulating capital, over a current assets or a class of assets both present and future, which lies dormant until crystallisation or winding-up).

There is a standard set of articles for a company limited by shares, which is termed "Table A". This table is contained in the First Schedule of CA 1963. If a company does not register articles of association then it will receive Table A by default. The Articles of Association must be signed by the subscribers and are registered with the Companies Registration Office. Once the Articles are registered they create a legally binding contract.

Any alteration to the articles must be by a special resolution of the members, and in accordance with section 15 CA 1963. However, the right to alter the articles is subject to such alteration not overriding the Companies Act, Memorandum of Association and general rules of law. Any alteration to the articles must be made *bona fide* and in the best interests of the company as a whole.

Form A1 – this form includes details of:

(a) the first Directors, and first Secretary of the Company (who must also sign the form),
(b) the address of the company's registered office,
(c) a Statutory Declaration by a solicitor engaged in the formation of the company or a person named as a Director or Secretary, stating that all the statutory requirements of the Companies Acts 1963–2009 (CA 1963–2009) have been adhered to,
(d) a statement of capital, detailing the classes of shares, nominal value and number of shares, authorised and issued.

If these documents are in order then a Certificate of Incorporation is issued. This document proves that:

(a) The company has been registered and the relevant date,
(b) Whether the company is public or private, and
(c) That the statutory requirements of the Companies Acts 1963-2009 have been complied with.

The Companies Consolidation and Reform Bill 2007 will remove the requirement for a company to have a separate Memorandum and Articles of Association, and replace them with a single document.

Types of Companies

There are three basic types of companies, which can be classified in accordance with the manner in which they are formed, namely:

1. Chartered Companies These were organisations created by a decree of the English Monarchy (royal charter) during the 19th Century and were mainly connected with education. Many chartered companies still exist in Ireland today, including:

- The Law Society of Ireland
- The Honourable Society of the Kings Inns
- Trinity College Dublin
- Royal College of Surgeons
- Bank of Ireland

Since Ireland's independence the Executive has assumed the power to grant charters, although it has never done so.

2. Statutory Companies These were companies granted their status by the authority of an Act of Legislature (other than the Companies Act), and traditionally they were conferred with special powers and monopolistic rights. Since independence most of these companies have been dissolved and their business dealings transferred to new State bodies. Previously formed statutory companies, whose objectives were considered to fulfill certain commercial functions of national importance, e.g.including Aer Lingus, have become public companies.

3. Limited Companies Companies may be limited by shares or by guarantee.

Companies Limited by Shares

The most common type of company is a limited liability company registered under the Companies Acts 1963–2009. These Acts proscribe the procedure to be followed before the Registrar of Companies can affect registration. A limited company can take two forms, namely either:

A. A Private company; or
B. A Public company.

A Private Registered Company is a company that has a share capital and which by its Articles of Association:

I. Restricts the right to transfer shares.
II. Limits the number of its members to a maximum of 99 and a minimum of one (under the EC (Single-Member Private Limited Companies) Regulations 1994.)
III. Prohibits any invitation to the public to subscribe for any shares or debentures in the company.

There is no minimum capital requirement for private companies, and small to medium-sized private companies are exempt from many of the procedural and publicity requirements in relation to accounts and returns. A private company can commence trading once a Certificate of Incorporation is obtained from the Companies Registrar. A Public Limited Company is a limited liability company that states in its Memorandum of Association that it is a public company and is registered as such. To constitute a PLC, minimum membership is seven members (section 5 CA 1963), and the name of the company must end with the words "public limited company", plc or "cuideachta phoibli teoranta". Public companies are required to have a minimum share capital of €38,092, at least 25% of which must be fully paid-up (section 5(2) CA (Amendment) 1983). This capital may be raised by offering shares and debentures to the public, subject to the rules set down by the Companies Act, European legislation and the rules of the Stock Exchange.

A public company may only commence trading once a Certificate of Incorporation and a Trading Certificate has been issued by the Companies Registrar.

Current Irish law is based on the model of the PLC, despite the fact that private limited companies are much more common. The Companies Consolidation and Reform Bill 2007 will make the "private company limited by shares or CLS" the model company within the Companies Acts.

4. Companies Limited by Guarantee If a company is limited by guarantee then it is prevented under section 7 CAA 1983 from being a public limited company. Therefore these companies are more usually non-profit making organisations that do not require a capital base, such as charitable organisations, property management companies or clubs, where the members agree to contribute a pre-determined amount to the assets of the companies upon winding up. Usually the members do not provide money to the company upon formation or during its life, therefore, it is suitable for companies that wish to obtain legal personality and limited liability but that do not need to raise money from their members. Additionally, an elected council or committee, instead of a Board of Directors, may carry out the management of a company limited by guarantee, if its members so decide.

5. Unlimited Companies Some unlimited companies still exist within the State, and members of these companies agree upon winding-up that they shall be liable, without limit, to contribute to the assets of the company a sufficient amount for the payment of the company's debts and liabilities. In reality unlimited companies are very rare in Ireland. They are usually formed by companies who do not intend to trade, such as companies formed for tax management purposes. In addition, these companies are exempted from many financial disclosure requirements and they do not have to pay capital duty on the registration of the company.

Characteristics of a Registered Company

Separate Legal Entity The Company is a separate legal person independent from its members or shareholders, as established by Salomon v. Salomon & Company Limited (1897) which ruled that "a company at law is separate from the persons who control it. As a separate legal artificial person, the company possesses certain rights and is subject to certain duties, similar to those of a human person. A company has the right to:

- Hold or own property
- Enter into contractual relations and conduct business in its own name
- Sue or be sued in its own name
- It must register with the Revenue Commissioners for the purpose of paying taxation.
- It has perpetual existence, i.e it lasts indefinately.

As an artificial entity, with no mind or body of its own, a company requires a natural person to act on its behalf. Accordingly management is vested in a Board of Directors which, as agents for the company, can bind the company by making and effecting decisions on its behalf.

Liability Most registered companies enjoy the privilege of limited liability. This liability may be limited either by shares or guarantee, see above. Generally, most profit-orientated companies are limited by shares. This in effect means that if a company is wound up then the creditors have no right of action against the members, and the member's liability is limited to the amount of their investment in the company. If part of the member's investment in the company is unpaid then they are liable to the company's creditors to the unpaid amount on their shares.

Personal Guarantees Despite the fact that the majority of companies in Ireland are limited liability companies, this does not mean that the shareholders have no liability in the event of insolvent liquidation. Where shareholders provide personal guarantees in return for borrowings they will be fully liable for all outstanding debt, even to the extent of their own personal bankruptcy. Personal guarantees are the means by which powerful lenders avoid the limited liability of the members of the company to which they lend money. Rather than merely rely on the capital of the company, the lenders require the members to enter into a contractual agreement that they will back the debts of the company with their own personal wealth. Effectively this device removes limited liability with respect to those lenders who are in a position to demand personal guarantees, although not ordinary trade creditors. In that way it undermines the theoretical effectiveness of limited liability by refusing to recognise it in practice.

Company Objectives The objects and powers of a company sare fixed by the Memorandum and Articles of Association, although both of these documents may be altered after the inception of the company in accordance with the Companies Act 1963-2009.

Publicity The Memorandum and Articles of the company, as well as all such documentation required to be registered from time to time, are open to inspection by the public on the payment of a nominal fee.

Size Generally PLCs are large commercial organisations as they have greater access to investment capital. Private companies end to be smaller businesses.

Company Management The members of the company, i.e. its shareholders are the owners of the company although they are not generally the persons responsible for the day to day running of the company. The company's directors assign this task to the company's management team and employees. These directors are responsible for the strategic planning and progress of the company, and their role is to oversee company growth and development. In a private company, directors are often substantial shareholders.

Subscription Every registered company must have at least two Directors and one Company Secretary (exemption for single-member private companies). The Companies Consolidation and Reform Bill 2007 will reduce the number of directors required in a CLS to one, although that director cannot simultaneously act as company secretary.

Perpetual Succession A company once formed will continue to exist up until such time as it is wound-up. The fact that a shareholder, even one holding a 100% share-holding, dies has no effect on the legal existence of the company. Registered companies can be further classified as follows:

Holding and Subsidiary Companies Sometimes companies are organised into a group. There will be one holding company that holds shares in other companies called "subsidiaries". Group companies are common where a company has a diverse series of interests or wants to separate its areas of business for management and administration reasons. A company is considered a holding company of another company under section 155 CA 1963 if:

1. It is a member of that company and controls the composition of its Board of Directors, or
2. It holds more than half the nominal value of that company's share capital or voting rights, or
3. The other company is a subsidiary of a subsidiary of the holding company.

Associated Companies An associated company is one in which a company is beneficially entitled to more than 20% of the nominal value of the ordinary shares of the company, or allotted share capital of the company.

Related Companies Under CA 1990 a company is related to another if:

(a) That other company is its holding company or subsidiary, or
(b) Another company holds more than half the nominal value of its equity share capital, or
(c) That other company exercises or controls more than 50% of the voting power at any general meeting, or
(d) The businesses of more than one company have been carried on in such a manner that it is impossible to separate them, or
(e) If there is another company to which both companies are related.

Single-member Private Companies These are companies with only one member (sole traders with limited liability), although they are currently still required to have two directors Under the EC (Single Member Private Company) Regulation 1994 (EC(smpc)R 1994), one person companies can dispense with the requirements of holding an AGM, passing resolution to amend the Memorandum or Articles of Association and quorums for company meetings.

Task 2: Response

MEMO

To: Jane Dough
From: Chris, Shield Kenwick
Re: Company vs. Sole Trader
Date: 1 January 2009

Setting up as a Sole Trader

"Sole Trader" is the term used to describe a business that is wholly owned by one person but not regulated by the Companies Acts 1963-2009. In other words, you would be the complete controller of the business' destiny. Up until the second part of the last century the sole trader was the traditional method of doing business in Ireland.

There is no specific law governing sole traders, rather a series of separate and disparate set of rules governing the area. The main characteristics of a sole trading business are:

(a) No formal permission is required to commence a business as a sole trader, although there are some ancillary business requirements depending upon the type of business being set up. For example, if you were to commence trading by using a name other than your own name, then such name must be registered under the Registration of Business Name Act, 1963 – this requirement applies to all types of business organisations. Another requirement is that you would be required to inform the local Inspector of Taxes that you have commenced business so that the Revenue Commissioner may issue you with a VAT number/Self Assessment Tax Certificate in due course.

(b) Generally sole traders operate as small businesses. This is mainly because their capital base would be limited by the personal resources of the owner and his/her success in the running of the business.
(c) The owner (i.e. you) would have exclusive responsibility for all decision making pertaining to the business.
(d) The owner would be accountable only to themselves i.e. you would have freedom of action and privacy in the running of the Dough House.
(e) There are few legal restrictions in setting up a business as a sole trader, therefore there is a greater degree of flexibility.

However, the following points should also be borne in mind before making a final decision:

As a sole trader, you would have no separate legal personality from your business and therefore may be personally sued on behalf of the business. Also, the concept of **unlimited liability** would be applied. Essentially this means that you would be wholly liable for all the debts of the business. Therefore, if the business fails or if there are insufficient funds to pay the businesses debts as they fall due then as owner you are completely liable for the businesses debt to the extent that you could be declared personally bankrupt by the courts.

You are likely to have **restricted scope for raising capital**. The main sources of capital available to you as a sole trader are your own personal savings, personal bank borrowing and accumulated profits from previous trading years, if available.

The "starting a business" section of the website www.basis.ie is a useful reference point to get information on many of these issues. In addition, I strongly advise that you meet with Mr Ryan, or your solicitor, to discuss this issue further before making a final decision. You may also wish to consider the formation of Single Member Private Limited Company under the Companies Acts 1963-2009 as an alternative to being a sole trader.

Task 3: Response

Briefing Note

To: Jane Dough
From: Shield Kenwick
Re: Partnerships

A partnership is defined by section 1 of the Partnership Act 1890 (PA 1980) as an association of two or more people carrying on a business together with a view to making a profit. Within a partnership all the partners pool their capital and management expertise and in return accept responsibility for the joint operation of the business. Essentially, a partnership is an unincorporated business organisation. In Ireland, partnerships are still a relatively common method of doing business. Section 4 of the 1890

Act provides that persons who enter into partnerships are to be collectively termed a "firm".

By virtue of the Partnership Act all partnerships require a minimum of two people. Up until 1907, where one of the partners in the partnership had limited liability, maximum number of partners was 20 for an ordinary business and 10 for a banking business. The reasoning being that if more than 20 persons wish to carry on a commercial business they should form a registered company for that purpose. This requirement was extended to all partnerships by the Companies Act 1963 (CA 1963), save for accountants' or solicitors' partnerships, where the maximum is 50 partners (the exemption applies as professional practices cannot be carried on by a registered company).

Deed of Partnership

As with sole traders, no formalities are required for the formation of a partnership. The relationship may come into existence when the parties make an express contract (this is generally known as the Deed of Partnership) or when they make an implied contract (through their conduct vis-á-vis each other). Generally, most partnerships are created by prior written agreement in the form of the Deed of Partnership. In this regard it is usually advisable to approach a solicitor with a view to entering into a Deed of Partnership. This Deed should provide for the following matters:

(a) The nature of the firm's business, the name of the firm and its principal place of business.
(b) The capital and property of the firm and the proportion in which it is contributed by each partner.
(c) The date of commencement and the intended duration of the partnership.
(d) Provision for the payment of salaries, if any, to the partners.
(e) Rights, obligations and duties of each individual partner i.e. the legal relationship between the different partners.
(f) Provision for audits and accounts.
(g) Provision for partner drawings.
(h) Provision for partnership meetings.
(i) Division of profits and losses.
(j) The procedure to be adopted on the death, retirement or bankruptcy of a partner.
(k) The procedure for the valuation of the goodwill and assets on the sale of the partnership or on the death of a partner.
(l) Provision for the dissolution of the partnership.
(m) Provision for the admission of an additional partner or the expulsion of an existing partner.
(n) An arbitration clause setting down the procedure to be used in solving disputes: the advantage of arbitration is that disputes are settled by an informal procedure in private and without the expense, formality and publicity of a court case. Arbitration procedure is governed by the Arbitration Act 1954–1980 (AA 1954–1980).

The Relationship of Partners with each other

Each party has a duty to act *bona fide* and in the best interest of the partnership once it is established. Consequently all partners are bound to render true accounts and full information on all matters affecting the partnership. In addition, all partners must account for any profits made by them without the consent of the others as a result of using the firm's name, property or trade connections.

In return each partner is entitled to access the partnership books and may take part in the management of the business.

Liability of Partners

Similar to the sole trader situation, each partner is jointly liable for all the debts and obligations of the firm incurred during the course of his/her partnership. This means that if you were to join a partnership, you and your partners would be jointly and severally liable for the debts of the partnership.

The Limited Partnership Act 1907 (LPA 1907) allows for one of the partners to have limited liability, but this fact must be registered with the Registrar of Companies under section 5 of the Partnership Act 1890 (PA 1890). The purpose of this registration is that persons dealing with the firm can easily ascertain who the partners are, and what their liability is. A limited partner is excluded from taking part in the management of the company, cannot bind the firm contractually, and cannot dissolve the partnership by notice, nor is the partnership dissolved by the death, bankruptcy or lunacy of that partner. A limited partner may inspect the firm's books, and may, with the consent of the other partners, assign his or her share of the partnership. The assignee then becomes subject to all the rights and liabilities of the limited partner.

The Investment Limited Partnerships Act 1994(ILPA 1994) creates specific rules for investment limited partnerships as created by that act.

Dissolution of a Partnership

Circumstances may arise where the partnership irretrievably breaks down or some other reason leads to the partnership being unable to continue. Dissolution is the procedure whereby a partnership is brought to an end, and may be specifically provided for in the Deed of Partnership. Where there are no express provisions then the Partnership Act 1890 applies with regard to dissolutions as follows:

(a) By retirement/notice given by a partner from a partnership at-will (a partnership for an undefined time). This can only be done where all the partners concur. Where one or more, but not all, wish a mutual dissolution it cannot be affected this way. Once all the partners agree, dissolution is effective from the moment of agreement, or from some other date agreed on. A dissolution by agreement may be verbally agreed.

(b) By the efflux of time, where the partnership was formed for a specific purpose/venture or for a pre-determined period.
(c) By the death or bankruptcy or any of the partners: this is because the partnership is not a distinct or separate legal person and therefore cannot exist apart from those members who compose it. As a result, the death or bankruptcy of a partner will normally bring the partnership to an end automatically. Therefore even though a partner might bequeath his share of the partnership to a third party upon his death, this transfer is ineffectual. This is because a partner's interests' cannot be transferred without the consent of the other partners – and thus all partnerships must be dissolved upon the death of any one partner.
(d) By an intervening illegality: an event which renders it unlawful for the business of the firm to be carried out/or if the partnership was formed for an illegal purpose then it was illegal *ab initio*.
(e) By an Order of the Court where:
　(i) A partner becomes permanently mentally ill, insane or incapable of managing his own affairs. This Order is made to preserve the incapacitated partner's interests.
　(ii) A partner suffers a permanent physical incapacity.
　(iii) A partner is guilty of misconduct that prejudicially affects the business. Misconduct in this instance refers to misconduct with regard to the business, though behaviour by a partner in his private life which reflects adversely upon the business may be sufficient.
　(iv) A partner wilfully and persistently breaks the partnership agreement.
　(v) If the business of the partnership can only be carried on at a loss.
　(vi) The court considers it just and equitable that the partnership be dissolved.

On the dissolution of the partnership any one of the partner may publicly provide notification of the dissolution.

Type of Partner

Generally a partnership can have two distinct types of partners, namely:

(a) An active partner who has full managerial and financial liability – this type of partner automatically assumes unlimited liability.
(b) A sleeping partner is a person who has no managerial liability and whose financial liability is agreed at a fixed sum under the Limited Partnership Act 1907. Essentially this partner contributes capital and takes a share of the profits without participating in the management of the business. The existence of this type of partner within a partnership agreement must be registered with the Registrar of Companies under section 5 of the Partnership Act 1890. The death, lunacy or bankruptcy of a limited partner does not necessitate the dissolution of the partnership.

Task 4: Response

Briefing Note

To: Jane Dough
From: Shield Kenwick
Re: Contracts of Employment and Health and Safety

Contracts of Employment

Any relationship between you (as employer) and your employees (whether family or not) should be governed by the contract of employment. Under that contract an employee agrees to render personal service to the employer in return for wages or other remuneration. Employment contracts are not required to be in writing, but under the Terms of Employment Information Acts 1994 to 2001(TEIA 1994 – 2001) employers are required to give employees a written document providing prescribed details of the terms of their employment (i.e. hourly rate, working hours, etc – see below). In effect, this is equivalent to a written contract of employment.

A contract of employment is usually a combination of express and implied terms. Express terms are those which are agreed in writing or orally and cover such aspects as rates of pay and overtime entitlements, pension entitlements, hours of work, the normal place of work, holiday entitlements, the right to take maternity, parental or adoptive leave, grievance and dispute resolution procedures, periods of notice on termination of employment and normal company rules.

However, further terms that may be added to such a document include:

(a) Probationary period (no longer than one year) – should also include an extension provision.
(b) Procedures in relation to absenteeism and tardiness.
(c) Procedures in relation to layoff and short time. This is not provided for in law, but where it is anticipated that such a situation may arise at any time, a clause may be inserted in the contract authorising it.
(d) Requirements regarding flexibility and interchangeability.
(e) Right of security, search and privacy.
(f) Company rules (including internet/telephone usage policies).
(g) Confidentiality agreement or restraint of trade clause.
(h) Compulsory retirement age.
(i) Data Protection procedures (see below).

In practice it is quite common for an employer to incorporate all general terms and conditions relating to the contract of employment into an employee handbook, which is presented to the employee with their contract on commencement of employment.

All contracts of employment should contain a clause stating that the employee accepts and agrees to be bound by all terms and conditions of employment. Once signed by all relevant parties, both the employer and employee should retain a copy of the contract.

However, the terms of the contract may also include implied terms. These are often unwritten or unspoken terms that are understood as being part of the contract. The main sources of implied terms in employment law include statute law, custom, common law and the constitution. In some cases the parties may, by an express provision, exclude these customary or common law implied terms, but in most cases the terms are implied irrespective of the wishes of the parties. It is not possible to exclude terms implied by statute or under the constitution.

Irrespective of whether the employment contract is in writing or oral, there is a statutory requirement imposed upon the employer to provide certain information to employees by virtue of the Terms of Employment (Information Act) 1994 to 2001. This legislation requires you (as employer) to give detailed written information to an employee with regard to their terms of employment. A new employee must, within two months of commencing employment (or within two months where the request is made by an existing employee), be supplied with a written copy of the following information:

(a) The full names of the employer and the employee.
(b) The address of the employer, the principal place of work, or if there is no fixed/main place of work, a statement that the employee is required/permitted to work at various places.
(c) The title of the job or the nature of the work.
(d) The date of commencement of employment, and in the case of a temporary contract, the duration of the contract/date that the contract expires.
(e) The particulars of pay, the rate and method of calculation, frequency of payment, overtime, commission, bonuses and their method of calculation.
(f) The particulars concerning hours of work and holiday entitlements.
(g) The particulars concerning incapacity, sick pay arrangements and pension schemes.
(h) The period of notice which must be given by both the employer and the employee for the termination of the employment contract.
(i) A reference to any collective agreements that directly affect the terms and conditions of the employment.

The statement of terms and conditions must be signed and dated by or on behalf of the employer. A copy of the statement should be retained by the employer during the period of the employee's employment and for a period of one year thereafter.

Altering Contractual Terms It is quite common that following the creation of the contract of employment, either or both of the contracting parties may wish to vary the terms of the contract. Any variation to the contract must arise by mutual agreement between you and your employee(s) or their representatives. Mutual agreement may be demonstrated by oral agreement to the new terms, by the signing of a new statement of terms and conditions or by the employee showing acceptance by working in compliance with the new terms (known as "acquiescence"). Neither party is at liberty to unilaterally alter the contract, except where the terms of the contract provide for unilateral alteration, and subject to the change being reasonable between the parties.

Health and Safety

You will have a duty to take all reasonable care to ensure the safety of your employees. The key duties are contained in the Safety, Health and Welfare at Work Act 2005 (SHWWA 2005) and the regulations made under the act. In brief, the employer has a duty to provide the employee with a safe place of work, including safe access to and from work, a safe system of system, proper training, proper equipment and competent co-workers. Other legislation applies to specific workplaces and work substances, e.g. chemicals. The Organisation of Working Time Act 1997 (OWTA 1997) requires an employer to provide rest breaks, as specified under the act.

Task 5: Response

SHIELD KENWICK

Letterhead Paper
Ms Jane Dough
11 Harbourville Road
Ballymack

Dear Ms Dough

Further to our previous discussion, I would like to highlight the particular issues you need to consider before employing your nephew or niece in the Dough Shop.

The Protection of Young Persons (Employment) Act 1996 (PYP(E)A 1996) impacts young people in employment and affords legislative protection to young workers under the age of 18. This act applies to all employees, including apprentices, agency staff, public sector, civil service, local government, the Gardai and the Defence Forces. It contains the following provisions, namely:

Minimum Age for Entry into Employment

The legislation prohibits the full-time employment of children until they have reached the minimum school leaving age. The Schools Attendance Act 1926 (SAA 1926) requires that children between the ages of six and 15 must attend school. As evidence of this fact the worker must produce Birth Certificate and the employer must obtain permission from the parent or guardian before employing a person aged 14-15. Employers must also maintain satisfactory records in this regard. The employment of people under the age of 15 is generally prohibited, although children over 14 are permitted to do light, non-industrial work, or complete work experience during school holidays, provided that it does not interfere with their schooling and is not harmful to health and normal development. The Minister may permit certain other forms of child employment, in the areas of cultural, artistic, sports or advertising activities.

Limitations on Working Hours

The employment of children between that age and 18 is permitted subject to limitations. Workers aged 14 cannot work for more than seven hours in a day or 35 hours in a week (only outside of school terms). Workers aged 15-16 can only work for a maximum of eight hours in a day, and 40 hours in any week. Workers aged 16-18 can only work for a maximum of nine hours in a day, and 172 hours in any four weeks, and 2000 hours in any year. Double employment i.e. working for more than two employers, is prohibited where the aggregate hours worked exceed the prescribed maximum.

Employees who work more than five days a week, and whose work on a Sunday exceeds three hours must be given at least 24 hours consecutive rest in every seven day period. Any spell of work must not continue for more than four hours (14-15) or four and a half hours (16-18) without a rest interval of at least 30 minutes. Workers are also entitled to 12 hours, consecutive break between working days.

Persons aged 14-15 cannot be employed from 8 pm to 8 am, persons aged 16-18 cannot be employed from 10 pm to 6 am (in certain areas of activity, as agreed by the Minister, this period is 11 pm to 7 am).

Breach of the act's requirements is a criminal offence, prosecuted summarily by the Minister or the employee's trade union. Employers found guilty of an offence under the act are liable on summary conviction to a fine of up to €1,904.61. Continuing breaches of the act can attract a fine of up to €317.43 a day.

The above is a summary of the main requirements governing the area of employment of young people. Should you have any further queries, please give me a call.

Yours sincerely

etc.

Task 6: Response

MEMO

To: Mike Smithers, MCL
From: Chris, Shield Kenwick
Re: **Contracts of Service –V- Contracts for Services**
Date: xx January 2009

In employment law, there is a definite distinction between a contract of service and a contract for services. A contract of employment means a "contract of service" and should be distinguished from a "contract for services".

Normally, an employee under a contract of service is employed on a continuous basis to do a series of recurring tasks, is paid on a regular basis and is subject to an employer's instruction as to how a job is to be done.

A person employed under a contract for services is not classified as an employee, and is better described as an independent contractor. An independent contractor is employed to do a fixed task for a fixed sum and while he is told what to do, he is not told how to do it.

This distinction between an employee and independent contractor is an important one, for the following reasons:

(a) Statutory protection is only afforded to employees and not to independent contractors, for example, the Redundancy Payment Acts and the Unfair Dismissals Acts only apply to employees.
(b) An employer is legally responsible for the actions/negligence of employees whereas the same assumption of liability does not attach to the actions of independent contractors, save in exceptional cases (this is known as vicarious liability).
(c) An employee receives preferential payments upon the liquidation of a company, whereas an independent contractor ranks as an unsecured creditor.
(d) Some employment rights only attach to employees, such as participation in work and social clubs, trade union representation or involvement in health insurance schemes.
(e) Tax is assessed under different schedules for employees and independent contractors, and the social welfare code distinguishes between them and allows the employee to qualify for a wider range of benefits.

A practical example of the difference between an employee and independent contractor can be seen in the case of a chauffeur and a taxi driver, both of whom provide a similar service. A chauffeur would generally be classified as an employee who has a contract of service with his employer, whereas a taxi driver would be classified as an independent contractor, who has a contract to provide services to his passengers. The employer of the chauffeur has ongoing legal responsibilities in relation to such issues as salary and conditions of employment, whereas the taxi driver's customers have no responsibilities apart from payment for the service.

However, sometimes the distinction is not so clear, and consequently the Irish Courts have developed a series of tests to help to determine the distinction.

It is worth noting that in determining the status of a worker, the Supreme Court has expressed the opinion that irrespective of the fact that the drafters of a contract have attached labels such as "employee" or "independent contractor" this will not preclude the Court from making a determination of the party's actual status based on a consideration of the totality of the relationship between the parties.

It is recommended that you consider carefully whether the proposed engagement for cleaning services is actually a contract of service or a contract for services.

Contracts

Should you decide that the engagement is a contract of service, and hence an employment, I recommend that you draw up an employment contract. The contract may be classified under a variety of different headings, including:

Permanent Contracts This is a contract of indefinite duration and contains no end date other than a final end date on retirement. It is however, capable of being terminated on the giving of the required statutory/contractual notice, provided the termination is in accordance with the Unfair Dismissals Act and complies with the constitutional requirement of fair procedures.

Temporary Contracts This type of contract may be used for a fixed term or for a specified purpose.

It should also be noted that the Unfair Dismissals Acts 1977 – 2007 (UDA 1977 – 2007) now contain anti-abuse provisions in relation to fixed term workers. In effect, section 3 of the Unfair Dismissals (Amendment) Act 1993 (UD(A)A 1993) states that where an employee is dismissed by reason of the expiry of a temporary contract, and the employee is subsequently re-employed within three months of the original contract's termination by the same employer and under a similar fixed term or specified purpose contract, and is re-engaged in similar or the same work, then the third party is entitled to conclude that the employer was seeking to avoid liability under the legislation, and the terms of the Unfair Dismissals Act will apply to any subsequent dismissal, and a possible redundancy situation may also exist.

Task 7: Response

MEMO

To: Jane Dough
From: Chris, Shield Kenwick
Re: **Landlord and Tenant Law: Lease of the Dough House**
Date: xx February 2009

A lease is (usually, but not always) a written document under which you, the tenant, holds land and/or buildings from a landlord. The lease will contain certain terms, conditions and covenants applicable to both the landlord and the tenant. In addition to these terms and conditions, the lease must contain lawful provisions. If an unlawful provision is contained in a lease, that provision and sometimes the lease in its entirety may be struck down as null and void. In addition to this, there are certain statutes that govern the area of commercial leases which operate to confer certain legislative and statutory rights on the holders of leases.

For example, if the lease exceeds five years in duration, as tenant you will be entitled to apply for a long lease. This is done pursuant to landlord and tenant legislation by way of the tenant serving on the landlord a document known as a Notice of Intention to Apply for Relief. This document puts the landlord on notice that the tenant is exercising their right to apply for a long lease. After this notice is served, usually, negotiations will begin between the landlord and the tenant surrounding the terms of the long lease (term, duration, rent, conditions, covenants etc). As stated above, a lease is a set of terms and conditions existing between a landlord and tenant. The conditions governing the relationship between the two is effectively a contract. It will provide for rent, due dates, and the various obligations on the part of the landlord and the tenant. These leases should be negotiated between the solicitor for the lessor/landlord and the solicitor for the lessee/tenant. It should be noted that, in your case, the landlord will be taking on certain responsibilities, i.e to fit out the premises. This should be reflected in the lease.

It is important to note that there may be stamp duty payable on the lease and a solicitor may be able to advise in this regard. Stamp duty is a duty levied by the Government and is a form of tax. On payment of this tax to the Revenue Commissioners, the document (lease) is "stamped" with the amount of the duty payable. If stamp duty is not paid, not only does the party to be charged render themselves liable to interest and penalties, but the lease is not a valid document in the eyes of a court in the event that it becomes the subject of a legal dispute. The client should be careful that there is provision in the lease to allow a coffee shop in the premises as a user, and no restrictions on opening hours, which might affect the proposed business.

Also, there may be planning considerations that will impact upon you. The premises may not be permitted to be used as a coffee shop, and you should enquire with a planning consultant or engineer as to whether you need to apply for planning permission to change the use from its previous designation to coffee shop.

Task 8: Response

FILE NOTE:

Client: MCL Limited
Re: Employee Records and Data Protection Legislation
Initials: Chris
Date: 2 February 2009

Under the Data Protection Acts 1988 to 2003 (DPA 1988 – 2003) a right of privacy exists in relation to data held on computers. Employers often become what is termed under the relevant legislation as a "data controller". A data controller is someone who controls and is responsible for the keeping and use of personal information on computer or in structured manual files. Employment contracts may contain such information and accordingly may be caught under the terms of the Data Protection Acts 1988 to 2003.

The Data Protection Acts are designed to keep information held about individuals (in this case employees) secure and confidential.

In general terms, MCL is required to:

1. Obtain and process the information fairly.
2. Keep it only for one or more specified and lawful purposes.
3. Process it only in ways compatible with the purposes for which it was given to them initially.

4. Keep it safe and secure.
5. Keep it accurate and up-to-date.
6. Ensure that it is adequate, relevant and not excessive.
7. Retain it no longer than is necessary for the specified purpose or purposes.
8. Give a copy of his/her personal data to any individual, on request.

Specific rules apply in relation to the collection and storage of "sensitive personal data". This includes information on issues such as ethnic origin, political opinions and sexual health. Of most importance to an employer is whether the data subject is a trade union member, and information about the physical or mental health of the date subject. These provisions are binding on every data controller. Any failure to observe them would be a breach of the Data Protection Acts. However, if Mike has any concerns, he would be advised to consult with a specialist solicitor in this regard. Mike should also be aware that the issue of employers monitoring employee behaviour, particularly use of the internet and through CCTV, is becoming an area of concern in Data Protection law.

Task 9: Solution

Briefing Note

To: Jane Dough
From: Shield Kenwick
Re: Phases of a Contract

There are three main elements to a contract, namely **offer, acceptance** and **consideration**. However, before a contract can be entered into, a person must have what is known in law as the "capacity to contract".

Capacity to Contract

Some persons are determined by law to be unable to contract freely. Generally when this person enters into a contract then the resulting contract may be declared invalid and hence unenforceable i.e. the parties cannot be bound to the contract that they have made. Examples of persons who may be unable to contract freely include infants and minors, convicts, mental incompetents and drunkards. It should be noted that a corporate body is a competent contracting party. The law recognises a company as a juristic entity separate and distinct from the natural persons who constitute the company. To obtain separate legal personality and limited liability companies are legally obligated to state their objectives upon formation in their Memorandum of Association. Thereafter corporations are only allowed to enter into contracts to achieve these objectives. Contracts entered into for purposes outside of these objectives are termed *ultra vires* contracts and are generally unenforceable.

Offer

An offer is an essential element of all valid contracts. In legal terms an offer can be defined as:

"a clear and unambiguous statement of the terms upon which the parties are willing to contract should the person to whom the offer is made decide to accept".

This offer statement can either be made orally, in writing, by electronic communication, or by conduct i.e. by bidding at an auction, by boarding a bus, by ordering a meal at a restaurant etc.

Generally offers can be classified as either unilateral offers or bilateral offers. A bilateral offer is an offer made to a specified person, whereas a unilateral offer may be addressed to a group of people or to the public at large.

In determining what is meant by an offer it is important to distinguish it from "an invitation to treat". An invitation to treat is merely an invitation to make an offer. In legal terms an invitation to treat is a statement made without any intention that a legal contract will result if the person indicates his ascent to those terms. Generally, an invitation to treat is a step prior to the bargaining process and the courts often view the response itself to be an offer, which can in turn accepted or rejected.

Termination of an Offer

An offer may be terminated in the following ways:

(a) By being **rejected**: This rejection may be expressed and implied. Express rejection occurs where the offeree simply rejects the offer. Implied rejection would be constituted by a counter-offer or a conditional acceptance. (See notes on acceptance.)
(b) By **withdrawal or revocation** at any time before it is accepted.
(c) By **lapse of time** (where the offer remains open for a specific period of time). In addition, where the offeror has not specified how long the offer will remain open, it will lapse after a reasonable length of time has passed. What the court will consider a reasonable period of time will depend on the goods/commodity in question, and all other relevant circumstances.
(d) Arising from **death.** If either party dies before acceptance can take place then there can be no contract.
(e) An offer may also be brought to an end where the offeree makes a **counter-offer** (see notes on acceptance).

Acceptance

Acceptance may be defined as "the final and unequivocal expression of agreement to the terms of the offer". Acceptance is usually in the same form as the offer, unless the offeror specifies a special method for acceptance. Acceptance may arise in a variety of ways, such as:

(a) **Performance** This only applies in cases of a unilateral offer. Acceptance by performance also occurs where the parties conduct themselves in such a manner as to indicate that they believed that the contract existed.
(b) **Communication of Acceptance** Communication of acceptance will generally take place by a verbal or written agreement (post, telegram, fax or e-mail).

Counter-Offer

A counter offer is a new offer which may result in acceptance. Essentially, where the response of the offeree is not a clear and unconditional acceptance of the offer the response itself may be described as a counter-offer that in turn may be accepted or ignored by the person to whom it is addressed.

It is important to note that an offeror can only waive the need for acceptance to be communicated to him; he cannot oblige the offeree to respond to the offer by stating that failure to communicate rejection of the offer will amount to consent.

For acceptance to be effective the general rule is that the offeror is bound when he learns from the offeree of their acceptance. At that moment the contract comes into existence. This also applies to communications via the telephone and fax. For example, A rings B and makes B an offer. B rings A back and before he has the opportunity to accept this offer the line goes dead. B must phone A again to make acceptance effective i.e. an offeror cannot be bound by silent acceptance.

A special rule applies for postal acceptance. For the purpose of contract law, the rule of acceptance is that an offer is accepted on the date and time it is sent by post and not at the date and time it is received by post. In **Sanderson v. Cunningham** (1919) the plaintiff, through a Dublin insurance broker, sent in a proposal/application form for an insurance policy to a London-based insurance company. This constituted an offer made by him to the insurance company. The insurance company decided to issue him with the insurance policy and posted it to him. The plaintiff read the policy, agreed with the terms contained therein and signed it. The plaintiff later made a claim against the policy, which the insurance company refused to pay out. The plaintiff wished to sue the insurance company but could only do so in Ireland if the contract was concluded in Ireland. The court held that the contract was concluded in Ireland as it was posted from Ireland to London.

In modern business, the postal rule is avoided by the parties specifying that it does not apply, or by using other methods of communication e.g. email.

Consideration

The third element of a valid agreement is consideration. The doctrine of consideration is based on the concept of "mutuality of obligation" and the concept of *quid pro quo*, the idea being that:

- Each party to the contract is under a legal duty to the other party to the contract.
- Each party to the contract has made a legally binding promise to the other party to the contract.
- Each party to the contract is under an obligation to the other party to the contract.
- Consideration involves some detriment to the promisee or some benefit to the promisor.

Essentially, both parties must give something and both parties must get something. Without consideration, a contract will not be enforceable. In simple terms, consideration is "the price that the promisee pays in return for the promise" – this price may be in terms of either money or monies-worth. This consideration must be real and genuine. The courts will not enforce a contract supported only by false or vague promises, such as praying for someone as opposed to paying them for goods or services received. In addition, consideration must also be legal. However, freedom of contract means that the parties can set any value they wish on the consideration, it need not be a fair price or even good value.

Discharge of Contractual Obligations

Every valid contractual obligation gives rise to a corresponding contractual right. Where the obligation of one party is fully discharged, the corresponding right of the other party is extinguished. When all rights and obligations are extinguished then the contract is discharged. A contract may be discharged in a variety of ways and contractual obligations are deemed to come to an end. Legal advice should be sought if this situation arises.

Task 10: Response

MEMO

To: Legal Department
From: Chris
Re: ICAI and CARB
Date: February 2007

As per Mr Ryan's instructions, please prepare a briefing note on the operation of CARB in the event that any complaint is made against this firm. The briefing note should cover the following areas:

- Liability of members, firms and affiliates.
- A summary of the bye-laws, regulations and codes governing chartered accountants in the carrying out of their functions, both professional and otherwise.
- A note of the various regulatory and disciplinary committees.

- Special Investigator and AIDB referral.
- Complaints handling process – Complaints Committee referrals.
- Disciplinary Tribunal referrals.

CARB's website can be found at www.carb.ie

Task 11: Solution

Briefing Note

To: Mike Smithers, MCL
From: Shield Kenwick
Re: Company Capital: Shares vs Loan

Company Capital

A company's capital is the money that it has available to trade with, and is the basic funding of the company. Depending on its source, capital can either be classified as share capital or loan capital. In other words, MCL could consider raising a loan to finance the company from its inception or raise money by issuing shares.

Share capital is the money that a company raises by borrowing from personal investors who purchase shares (or a share) in the company. Therefore, the members (otherwise known as the shareholders) of a company consist of those parties who have subscribed for shares in the Memorandum of Association, and others who have agreed to become members and whose names have been entered in the company's Register of Members. A party may do this by agreeing to take an allotment of shares from a company, or by taking a transfer of shares from existing members. In either case entry on the Register of Members is a pre-requisite of membership.

Loan capital generally refers to company borrowing, whether through credit institutions or the issuing of debentures.

The original allotment of shares occurs when the company is formed and the subscribers agree in the Memorandum to take shares. The allotment of shares is a binding contract between the company and the subscriber. Once a subscriber is entered onto the Register of Members, he will then legally become a member of the company. When these shares are actually issued to the subscriber a share certificate evidences this issue.

A company's share capital main be classified as follows:

(a) **Nominal/Authorised Share Capital** This is the total amount of shares that a company has the authority to issue, either at formation or at a subsequent date. This amount is pre-determined in the Memorandum of Association.
(b) **Issued/Allotted Share Capital** This is the nominal value of shares that the company has already issued or allotted (or sold). A company is not required to allot all of its

share capital, and most companies reserve the right to issue shares at a later date to raise capital as it is required. The un-issued portion of a company's nominal share capital is known as "un-issued capital".

In Ireland it is common for companies to have a large figure for their nominal/authorised share capital, of which a much smaller amount is issued/allotted. In addition, a company can increase the nominal/authorised share capital figure in its Memorandum of Association by a simple resolution of 50% of the shareholders.

(c) **Called-up/Paid-up Share Capital** This is the value of shares that members have paid to date, where shares are being paid for in instalments. The remaining money per share that each shareholder owes to the company is known as the "uncalled capital".

(d) **Reserve Capital** This is uncalled capital that is reserved for a special purpose. Under section 67 CA 1963 a company may pass a special resolution stating that some or all of the uncalled capital may only be called up when the company is being wound-up.

Shares

If MCL is considering raising capital by way of shares, the following points should be noted. Shares may be defined as the interests of a shareholder in a company measured by a sum of money. The purchase of shares is a contract between the company and its shareholders consisting of a series of rights and obligations. A company may in either its Memorandum of Association or Articles confer different rights on different classes of shares. Companies may issue more than one class of shares. It is usual for the capital of a company to consist of two classes of shares, namely Ordinary Shares and Preference Shares. Different classes of shares have different class rights and these can be summarised as follows:

(i) *Preference Shares:* These are shares that usually give shareholders a prior right to receive a fixed dividend, and a preferential right to the return of capital upon the winding up of the company. Preference shareholders generally do not have voting rights at company meetings. Due to the fixed dividend, preference shares are an attractively safe investment option in comparison with ordinary shares where the rate of dividend will fluctuate depending upon company profits. With preference shares the payment of dividends is presumed to be cumulative. This means that if a dividend is not paid in a particular year because of a lack of profit, the arrears will be paid as soon as profits allow.

(ii) *Ordinary Shares:* These are the equity shareholders of the company and give the holders full members' rights. These shareholders bear the true burden of the company's fortunes, as their return on their investment is dependent upon the company's financial performance. The general rights of ordinary shareholders include: (1) voting rights at a general meeting, (2) the right to receive a dividend as fixed by the Board of Directors (which will fluctuate depending upon the profits made by the company), and (3) the right to participate in the distribution of capital upon the winding-up of the company, once all the company's debts have been paid.

(iii) *Redeemable Preference Shares:* These are shares that the company issues with the intention of redeeming them (buying them back) at some date in the future at a fixed rate.

(iv) *Bonus Shares:* This is where the company applies its reserves to paying up un-issued shares which are then allotted to existing members by way of a bonus.

(v) *Deferred Shares:* In the past companies allotted deferred or founder shares to the founders of the company. These shares carried special rights such as the right to receive a fixed dividend. However, these rights were deferred in priority to the ordinary shares. Today, these shares are rarely, if ever, issued.

Task 12: Solution

Briefing Note

To: Mike Smithers, MCL
From: Shield Kenwick
Re: Directors of companies: Rights and obligations

Companies, as artificial persons, cannot manage themselves. Therefore, the Articles of Association usually provide for the delegation of the management of the company to a Board of Directors. Directors are the human agents who have the powers and responsibilities for the day-to-day management of the company. In theory, the ownership and management of a company are separate functions to be performed by separate people. The company is owned by the shareholders and managed by the directors. However, as the majority of Irish companies are private this distinction is often more theoretical than practical, and the majority of shareholders will probably be directors of the company, company employees or the company secretary. This is currently the case with MCL. From a legal perspective a director is defined as any person involved in the management of a company. Section 174 CA 1963 provides that every company must have at least two directors, although the Articles may provide for well above the statutory minimum.

The Companies Consolidation and Reform Bill 2007 will reduce the number of directors required in a Company Limited by Shares to one (although that director cannot simultaneously act as company secretary).

A director is an office holder, and as such is not necessarily an employee of the company.

Types of Directors

(a) **Executive and Non-Executive Directors** An executive director is someone who manages the company on a full-time basis. This director is often an employee of the company or is employed under a contract for services. A non-executive director is someone who manages the company on a part-time basis. Such a person is often a director of the company because of his expert knowledge, experience, attainments and skills. In the case of MCL, Matthew and Maureen Smithers are considered non-executive directors.

The Companies Consolidation and Reform Bill 2007 will abolish the distinction between executive and non-executive directors required.

(b) **Managing Director** This is the director to whom the Board of Directors has delegated power to carry on the day-to-day management of the company. The Managing Director is an agent of the company and will have the authority to bind a company to all contracts. Generally, the Managing Director is given the responsibility of ensuring that the objectives and policies formulated by the Board of Directors are implemented. The powers of a Managing Director may be revoked, or the appointment terminated, by the Board of Directors if it sees fit. A company may be liable in damages if the appointment of a Managing Director is prematurely terminated, either as a consequence of an alteration of the Articles or pursuant to statute, if this action is inconsistent with his contract of service. Matthew jnr fulfils the role of Managing director in MCL.

(c) **Director for Life** This is a position exclusive to a private company and is normally a reward to an entrepreneur who has made a contribution to society through the creation of jobs and the payment of taxation.

(d) **Alternate Director** This is in effect a substitute director who can attend and vote at meetings when another director cannot. It is useful in cases of prolonged absences by a director, as a result of an illness or travel. A fellow director may be appointed as an alternate director, or an outsider may be appointed. Such an appointment is subject to revocation by the Board or the company in a general meeting.

(e) **Nominee Director** A nominee director is appointed to a company on the nomination of a powerful outsider, such as a major shareholder or creditor. Such a person does not have the right to appoint a director, but the company may agree to the request. The nominee director has a fiduciary duty to the company, himself and his nominator.

Appointment and Removal of Directors

(a) **Appointment** When a company is incorporated Form A1 is used to state the names of the first directors and secretaries of the company. All subsequent appointments are governed by the Articles of Association. In a private company the names of directors are often stated in the Articles of Association. Section 181 CA 1963 provide that a director may only be appointed individually, and the procedure is to be provided in the Articles of Association. Generally, they are appointed by an ordinary resolution of the shareholders at a general meeting or by a resolution of the Board to fill a casual vacancy or appoint an additional director. Section 28 CA 1990 limits directors service contracts to a maximum of five years.

The Companies Consolidation and Reform Bill 2007 requires newly appointed directors to sign a statement upon appointment, acknowledging their legal obligations.

(b) **Retirement** Retirement is by a process of rotation, under Article 92 Table A. At the first AGM all directors must retire and thereafter each year at the AGM one third of the company's directors must offer to resign. (This provision excludes the Managing Director and a director for Life). Those retiring shall be those longest in office since the last election and retiring directors are eligible for re-election. A director opting

for re-election shall be deemed to be re-elected unless the meeting decides otherwise. The aim of the rotation is to ensure that directors do not become too comfortable in their positions and that they realise that they hold their positions at the discretion of the shareholders.
(c) **Resignation** A director may resign by giving notice in writing to the company or by not offering himself for re-election.
(d) **Casual Vacancy** A casual vacancy may arise in a company. This is a vacancy that arises between an AGM, maybe due to death or resignation. This vacancy may be filled by the remaining directors co-opting a person to sit on the Board until the next election.
(e) **Removal** A director may be removed from the company by an ordinary resolution of the members. The company is required to provide its members with an extended 28 days notice in respect of any such resolution. Directors of private limited companies appointed for life by the Memorandum and Articles of Association can only be removed if the correct procedure for the alteration of the company's constitutional documents is followed and such removal complies with the requirements of natural justice.

Task 13: Solution

Briefing Note

To: Mike Smithers, MCL
From: Shield Kenwick
Re: Role of Company Secretary

The Company Secretary

Section 172 CA 1963 states that every company must have a company secretary. This secretary may also be one of the directors, but may also be a corporate body. If the secretary is also a director then anything required to be done by a director and a secretary cannot be done by the same person acting in a dual capacity as director/secretary. In practice this is rarely a problem, as the company must have two directors.

Appointment

The first Company Secretary is deemed appointed by including their name in the Memorandum or Articles of Association. The first Company Secretary must be named in Form A1, which is part of the company's registration documentation. Subsequent appointments are at the discretion of the directors or the shareholders, and they may also remove the secretary. Under Article 113 Table A "... the secretary shall be appointed by the directors for such term, at such remuneration, and upon such conditions as they may think fit, and any person so appointed may be removed by them".

There are no qualifications or disqualifications specified in the Companies Acts for the secretary of a private company, save that a restricted or disqualified person is prohibited from acting as a company secretary. However, section 236 CA 1990 provides that it is the duties of the directors in a public limited company to ensure that the company secretary possesses the requisite knowledge and experience, as well as appropriate qualifications, namely:

A. They were acting in the capacity of company secretary, deputy secretary or assistant secretary when the 1990 Companies Act was enacted, or
B. They were a company secretary for three of the previous five years, prior to their present appointment, or
C. The directors must be of the view that the person seeking to act as a company secretary is capable of discharging their functions based upon their experience or professional membership, or
D. The person must be a member of a relevant professional body recognised by the Minister for Enterprise Trade and Employment.

The Companies Consolidation and Reform Bill 2007 will require newly appointed company secretaries to sign a statement upon appointment acknowledging their legal obligations.

Duties The duties of the Company Secretary are not defined by legislation, and thus they will vary from company to company. In general a secretary's duties are administrative and not managerial. Essentially the role of the Company Secretary is to ensure that the company complies with the requirements of the Companies Acts. Their specific duties may include the following:

1. To keep charge of the statutory registers, including the Register of Members, Shares, Debenture Holders, Registers of Directors and Secretaries, and their shareholdings.
2. To make the annual returns to the Registrar of Companies.
3. To notify the Registrar of any changes to either the Memorandum or Articles of Association.
4. To witness all use of the company seal.
5. To give all members due notice of company meetings.
6. To keep the minutes of all general meetings and Board meetings.
7. To file details of all changes with the Registrar of Companies.
8. To correspond with shareholders regarding share calls, transfers, forfeitures and otherwise, and to ensure that interest and dividends payments are made correctly.
9. To be fully aware of the provisions of the Articles of Association and oversee that the directors act within their capacity, as specified by the objects clause.
10. To ensure the completion of all appropriate forms and their filing with the Companies Registrar when the company is converting to another type of company.
11. To compile a statement of affairs upon the appointment of a Receiver or Liquidator.

A Company Secretary is often the chief administrative officer of a company, and therefore has the usual power, and the apparent authority, to bind the company as its agent in day-to-day contracts. This power may be provided either expressly or implicitly in the Articles of Association.

The Companies Consolidation and Reform Bill 2007 provides that the duties of a Company Secretary will be those delegated by the Board of directors, which will increase the role of the Company Secretary.

Task 14: Solution

Briefing Note

To: Mike Smithers, MCL
From: Shield Kenwick
Re: Auditors: Responsibilities, Appointment and Removal

Auditors

As part of the Companies Acts every company must have an auditor whose duty it is to analyse the annual accounts and ensure that they provide a true and fair account of the company's financial affairs. Essentially, an auditor is an independent professional who examines the books and financial records of the company.

The relationship between an auditor and a company is not one of employer and employee. Instead the relationship is one of professional independent accountant and client. However, the auditor will be treated as an officer of the company for the purpose of imposing both criminal and civil sanctions in the event of fraudulent or reckless trading – this is akin to professional negligence in the law of tort.

To be an auditor the person must be suitably qualified, registered, independent, and not subject to any disqualification.

Qualifications

Section 187 CA 1990 sets out a list of persons who are qualified to act as the company auditor. Either a duly qualified individual or a firm may be so appointed (partnership). In essence, these people must be members of an accountancy body recognised by the Minister of Enterprise, Trade and Employment under the Companies Act 1990 as amended by the Companies (Auditing and Accounting) Act 2003 (C(AA)A 2003) as follows:

- A member of any of the following recognised accounting bodies, namely, ACCA (Chartered Association of Certified Accountants), ACA (Institute of Chartered Accountants

in Ireland, England, Wales and Scotland), IIPA (Institute of Incorporated Public Accountants in Ireland) or CPA (Institute of Certified Public Accountants in Ireland).
- Training, trained or qualified with any of the recognised accounting bodies.
- Authorised by the Minister before 3 February 1993, and is for the time being authorised by the Minister to act.
- Authorised by the Minister to be a practising member of an accountancy body, recognised under the Companies Act 1963, and under the law of another country.

The purpose of these qualifications is to ensure that the auditor is independent from the company's directors, is professionally competent and honest.

Section 72 of the Company Law Enforcement Act 2001(CLEA 2001) provides that a company director may demand that a purported auditor produce evidence of his qualifications. Failure to do so is an offence.

Registration

A qualified auditor must be registered with the Registrar of Companies under section 198 CA 1990, as amended by C(AA)A 2003, and the Registrar is obliged to maintain a register of the names and addresses of persons who he has been informed are qualified for appointment as an auditor. Particulars of each member qualified for appointment as auditor of the company are submitted to the Registrar on an annual basis. This is one of the conditions of recognition for accountancy bodies.

Each of the recognised bodies is also required to submit an annual report to the Minister giving details of the number of complaints received and the number and outcomes of cases dealt with by its investigation, disciplinary and appeals committees pertaining to members practising as auditors in the State.

The following persons are automatically disqualified from acting as a company auditor under section 187 CA 1990, as amended by C (AA)A 2003:

- An officer or servant of the company.
- An ex-officer or ex-servant of the company, within a period in respect of which accounts would be audited by them if they were appointed auditor.
- A parent, spouse, brother, sister or child, partner or employee of an officer of the company.
- A person who is disqualified from being an auditor of the company's holding or subsidiary company.
- Any former directors who are subject to a disqualification order.
- A body corporate (this is to ensure that accountants do not form companies, but remain trading in partnerships).

Furthermore, a person is prohibited from acting as an auditor of any company if the court has disqualified him in pursuance of the Companies Acts. To take up such an appointment would amount to committing a criminal offence.

Appointment

Section 160 CA 1963 states that the first auditor of the company is appointed by the directors before the first AGM, and holds office until that meeting. If the directors fail to make the appointment then the general meeting can make the appointment. At this first AGM the auditor is required to retire and will be re-appointed automatically without any resolution being passed, unless:

- The auditor is not qualified for re-appointment.
- The auditor does not wish to be re-appointed and has provided prior written notice to the company of this fact.
- A resolution has been passed to appoint another person as auditor.

Where an auditor is re-appointed at an AGM he thereafter holds office until the conclusion of the next AGM. The directors also have the capacity to appoint a person to act as auditor to fill a casual vacancy arising during the year, and the remuneration of the auditor is fixed by the directors.

If there is a general meeting at which the accounts are laid but no appointment of an auditor is made then the company must within one week give notice of the vacancy to the Minister who may then appoint a person to fill that vacancy. Failure to notify the Minister renders the company, and every officer in default, liable to a fine.

Removal

The auditor may voluntarily resign, or be removed or replaced against his wishes. Section 160 CA 1963 provides that an auditor may be removed from office by an ordinary resolution, requiring 28 days extended notice to members. A copy of this resolution must be sent to the Companies Registrar within 14 days and to the auditor whose removal is intended. An auditor who is nominated for removal has certain rights, may contact the company and shareholders for the purpose of canvassing for his reappointment, and may attend the relevant company meeting or make a representation in writing to the company. If this representation is received in advance of the meeting then it should be circulated to all members. An auditor is also entitled to have his representation sent to company members at the company's expense. The underlying intention of these rights is to guard a company against removing an auditor who has uncovered information that the directors would prefer to keep from the shareholders.

An auditor may also voluntarily resign from his post during his term in office if he serves a written notice to the company stating his intention to resign. Section 185 CA 1990 gives the auditor the power to resign and to either state, in his notice, that there are no circumstances connected with the company, or to state the circumstances connected with the company that should be brought to the attention of members and creditors. If there are circumstances to be brought to the attention of members or creditors, the company must notify every person entitled to receive a copy of the accounts and the Registrar of

Companies. An auditor who resigns in such circumstances is empowered to requisition an extraordinary general meeting (EGM) to consider his or her accounts and explanation of resignation.

Auditor's Power and Duties

Under section 193 CA 1990 the auditor has the following powers:

A. The right to access all written information regarding the books, accounts and vouchers of the company.
B. The right to ask questions/request explanations of the company's employees and officers.
C. The right to attend/receive notice and documents in relation to all general meetings.
D. The right to be heard at such meetings on any matter that concerns them as auditor.

Section 197 CA 1990 imposes severe criminal penalties upon company officers (including employees) who are convicted of giving false or misleading information to company auditors, or who fail to provide any information or explanations required by the auditors within two days of the request, save where it is not reasonably possible to comply.

In addition, they have the following duties:

A. **Duty to Investigate** The auditor is obliged, as part of his statutory duties, to investigate the financial affairs of the company and report to the members on these affairs at the AGM. In this regard the auditor is required to be alert to any wrongdoings, but is not necessarily required to seek them out. If the auditor is suspicious about something that is relevant he must enquire and satisfy himself as to whether his suspicions are justified. In some circumstances an auditor may be under a duty to seek legal advice where he comes across a matter in the course of an audit in respect of which he lacks specialist knowledge.

B. **Duty to Report to Members** Section 163 CA 1963 states that the auditor must report to the members on the accounts examined by them, and on every balance sheet, profit and loss account, and all group accounts laid before the company in general meetings during his/her term of office, as well as on the Director's Compliance Statement. The auditor must state that in his opinion the accounts reflect the company's true and fair financial position.

The Auditor's Report, which must be read at the AGM and must be open to inspection by any member, must contain the following information:

I. That all the necessary information and explanations, which to his best knowledge and belief is necessary for the purpose of the audit, has been obtained.
II. That in his opinion proper books of accounts have been maintained by the company.

III. That in his opinion proper returns were received.
IV. That in his opinion the balance sheet and profit and loss account are in agreement with the company's accounts and returns.
V. That in his opinion the company's balance sheet and profit and loss account have been prepared in accordance with the Companies Acts and provide a true and fair view of the company's financial affairs.
VI. That the auditor has reviewed the Director's Compliance Statement, and in his opinion it is fair and reasonable and provides a true and fair review of the company's financial affairs.
VII. Whether, in his opinion, there exists a financial situation that necessitates convening an extraordinary general meeting i.e. maintenance of capital provisions. Under CAA 1983 auditors are now required to comment on profits available for distribution, allotment of shares by a public limited company for non-cash consideration, or the transfer of a non-cash asset to a public limited company by a shareholder.
VIII. Particulars of any transactions involving directors, which have not been disclosed in the notes to the accounts.
IX. Whether, in his opinion, the information given in the Directors' Report is consistent with the accounts prepared for that year.

The content of the auditor's report must be accurate, precise and unequivocal.

C. **Duty to Act with Professional Integrity** Section 193 CA 1990 requires the auditor to be aware of their duties under the relevant legislation and the company's Articles of Association, although they are not necessarily required to have legal expertise. They must comply with the maintenance of auditing standards set by the professional accounting bodies.

D. **Duty of Care & Skill** If the auditor fails to perform his duties with reasonable care and skill, he may be liable to the company for his acts of negligence. The mere verification of the numerical accuracy of the accounts does not discharge this duty. The auditor must ensure that omissions and untruths are not made and irregularities are verified.

The auditor has a duty to the company in contract based upon the terms of his contractual relationship, but also a potential duty to all third parties in tort. This duty in tort arises provided there is sufficient proximity between the parties, the statement was made in a professional capacity and relied upon as such, and where an actual loss occurs. Several cases exist to support any investigation in this regard.

E. **Duties in relation to the maintenance of proper books of account** An auditor must have a qualified opinion if there are circumstances that require certain information to be brought to the attention of the company. Section 74 CLEA 2001 requires that where the books are not being kept in the manner required by the Companies Acts, and the contravention is neither minor nor immaterial in nature, the auditors must serve a notice on the company "as soon as practicable" stating their opinion to this effect. Furthermore, they must, within seven days of serving the notice, notify the

Registrar of Companies of the default, as well as the Office of the Director of Corporate Enforcement. Failure to do so amounts to a criminal offence for which penalties will be imposed. Where the directors rectify the situation or where the contravention is minor and immaterial in nature, the auditors do not have to proceed with notification to the Registrar.

F. **Duties under the Finance Act** Section 172 of the Finance Act 1995 imposes a duty upon the company auditor, where he is aware that the company has committed or is committing a taxation offence, to communicate that offence to the company and to request the company to take action to rectify the matter, and notify an officer of the Revenue Commissioners. Unless the auditor is satisfied that the company has done this within six months of the issuance of the notice, then he must resign. His resignation is effective by giving notice to the designated officer of the company, and he must cease to act as an auditor for a period of three years, or until they are satisfied that the necessary notification of the offence has taken place. Failure to comply with this requirement renders the auditor liable, on summary conviction to a fine not exceeding €1,270, and on indictment to a fine not exceeding €6,350, two years imprisonment or both.

G. **Duties under the CLEA 2001** Section 194(4) CA 1990 and section 74 of the CLEA 2001 provides that where an auditor comes to the opinion that a company or its officers or agents have committed an indictable offence under the Companies Acts, it must notify the Office of the Director of Corporate Enforcement. providing details. Compliance with this section is not regarded as a contravention of an auditor's professional or legal duties.

H. **Duties under the Companies (Auditing and Accounting) Act 2003** This Act created the Irish Auditing and Accounting Supervisory Authority (IAASA) as an independent regulatory body, whose principal function is to strengthen the regulation of auditors, and the methods by which supervisory bodies monitor their members.